THE HILL TRIBES
OF THAILAND

D1178218

Fourth Edition
30 [th] Anniversary of
Tribal Research Institute
1995

Technical Service Club
Tribal Research Institute

The Hill Tribes of Thailand

© Technical Service Club
Tribal Research Institute
All Rights Reserved

First Edition 1986
Second Edition & Revised 1989
Third Edition 1989
Fourth Edition
Revised & Enlarged 1995

Published by   **Technical Service Club**
Tribal Research Institute
Chiang Mai University campus
Chiang Mai 50200 Thailand
Tel. (053) 221933
Fax. (053) 222494

Revised by Mongkol Chanbamrung, Thaworn Foofuang
Design by T. Foofuang & P.Palalert
Photographs by Vichien Kacha-ananda, Pongkrit Palalert
Type by Suwalee Maneewan, Aworn Maneewan

Printed by   Nantakarn, Chiang Mai, Thailand.
Tel. (053) 410009, 217014

ACKNOWLEDGEMENTS

Technical Service Club would like to extend the special thanks to the following persons for their cooperation and assistance in the invaluable advice :

1. *Dr. John Mckinnon*
    Department of Geography
    Victoria University of Wellington
    New Zealand

2. *Dr. Christina Lammert Fink*
    Doctor of Philosophy in Anthropology
    University of California at Burkeley
    U.S.A.

*

CONTENTS

Introduction 1
- Affiliation, Distribution
  and size of population 3
- Socio-Economic patterns 6

Karen 13

Hmong 16

Lahu 22

Yao 25

Akha 31

Lisu 34

Lawa 36

Khamu 38

Mlabri 44

Provinces with Hill Tribe Settlements 47

Hill Tribe Settlements 48

Classification of Hill Tribes by -

Agricultural Practice 49

Calendar of Opium-Poppy Growing Tribes 50

Farm Calendar of Non Opium-Poppy

Growing Tribes 51

Traditional Socio-Agricultural Calendar

of the Hill Tribe in Thailand 52

Tribal Population Summary in Thailand 54

Some Sound Advice for Hill Tribe Trekkers 60

Hill Tribe Problem 64

Hill Tribe Policy 71

INTRODUCTION

In Thailand the term "hill tribes" designates ethnic minorities, most of whom live in the remote highland areas of the north and southwestern parts of the country. These people first attracted the serious attention of the Thai Government in 1959 when the National Committee for the Hill Tribes was set up.

There are many governmental and non-governmental agencies working with the hill tribes. These include military and civilian organizations, a few specialized United Nations agencies, and private voluntary organizations such as, and most important of all, the Royal Development Project for the Hill Tribes.

The present policy of the Thai Government towards the hill tribes is based on the Cabinet's decision July 6,1976, which states the government's intention to integrate these people into the Thai state and give them full rights to practise their religions and maintain their cultures. The principal objective of this policy is clear. It is stated quite precisely that the Thai Government wishes to enable the hill tribes to be first class, self-reliant Thai citizens.

There are many **hill tribe problems** as identified by Thai authorities. Most of these problems are related to some aspects of the hill tribes way of life which are considered to be inappropriate to the present socio-economic and political situation of the country.

It is widely believed that the type of shifting cultivation (swiddening) practised by most of the hill tribes causes deforestation and the deterioration of highland watersheds. Some tribes engage in opium production, and opium addiction is also a problem. The Hill Tribes also have less access to educational services, suffer poorer health and earn lower incomes when compared with other sectors of the national population. Moreover, as tribal groups living in relative cultural isolation, they lack a sense of national identity. This makes it much easier for cultural misunderstandings to occur and to be labelled as political infiltration and insurgency.

AFFILIATION, DISTRIBUTION AND SIZE OF POPULATION

Highlanders, as these people are sometimes called, fall into three linguistic stocks as in the following diagram.

Linguistic Classification of Hill Tribes in Thailand.

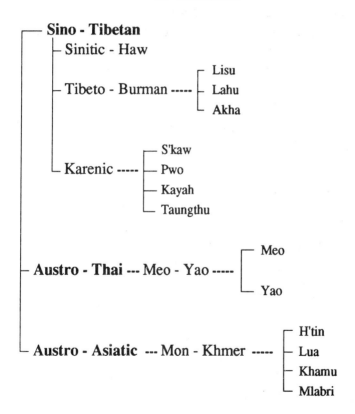

(*Source* : Matisoff, James A. in McKinnon & Wanat **Highlanders of Thailand,** 1983 : 65)

Apart from the above linguistic classification, these people can be divided into two groups according to their geographic distribution.

First, the low-hill and high-valley peoples consist of the Karen,Lua, Khamu and H'tin. These peoples do not traditionally grow the opium poppy.Generally speaking,they practise an ecologically-informed mode of cyclical shifting cultivation. They (the Lua and the Karen) prefer, where feasible, to develop wet rice fields. These are well established people who are considered to be indigenous to Thailand and the adjoining areas of Burma and Laos.

The second group is the pioneer swiddeners and the highland dwelling opium poppy growing peoples. They live at higher altitudes because the opium poppy only grows well above the 1,000 metre contour (above sea level). Included in this group are the Meo, Yao, Lahu, Lisu, and Akha,all of whom migrated into Thailand (from Burma and Laos) within this century.

The present highland population in Thailand is scattered over 20 provinces and 75 districts. Total population figures have been collected by the Tribal

4

Research Institute since the mid 1970s, and in the year 1995, the total was 694,720. The Karen are the largest group, and the Khamu are the smallest. The latest population figures in 1995 (Collected by Tribal Research Institute) are reflected in the following charts.

TRIBAL POPULATION

Tribes	Villages	Households	Persons	Percentage
Karen	2,132	60,385	321,900	46.34
Meo	243	16,146	124,211	17.88
Lahu	421	13,307	73,252	10.54
Akha	258	8,050	48,468	6.98
Yao	173	5,525	40,371	5.81
H'tin	148	6,090	32,755	4.71
Lisu	135	4,802	27,899	4.02
Lua	53	2,923	15,711	2.26
Khamu	32	1,988	10,153	1.46
Total	3,595	119,216	694,720	100

The above population figures exclude the "Palong" and the "Mlabri". The Palong are an ethnic group which just migrated to Chiang Mai Province in Thailand. There are presently 4 villages with a total of 90 households and 485 persons. The Mlabri, who are huntergathers, are a very small group estimated to consist of not more than 182 persons. They live in Phrae Province and Sa and Na Noi district of Nan Province.

SOCIO-ECONOMIC PATTERNS

It can be said that highlanders belong to the peasantry. In terms of their cultivation practices, they can be divided into three groups : dry rice cultivators, wet or irrigated rice cultivators, and a combinations of these. There are also three principal forms of land use :

1. Pioneer or primary swiddening,shifting cultivation in the real meaning where farmers move from place to place.

2. Land rotation of cultivable fields, sometimes called cyclical bush fallow. This system is based on permanent residence and can be said to be a stable or permanent form of agriculture.

3. Wet rice cultivation.

Pioneer swiddening is usually employed by opium-poppy growing people who can also be considered as a cash crop-oriented sector of the peasantry. The second type of land use, the rotational farming system, is practised by the Karen, Lua, H'tin and Khamu, who do not traditionally grow opium. This rotational system does not exhaust soil fertility and operates within fixed village boundaries. The Karen and the Lua also construct wet-rice terraces in the lowlands, uplands,and high valleys. (wherever there is sufficient water for irrigation).

Akha house

Cultivation

Harvesting

To sum up, on the one hand, the non-opium poppy-growing people practise a relatively stable system of agriculture and grow mainly ricc and a variety of other crops, primarily for home consumption with a little surplus for sale. On the other hand, the pioneer swiddeners and poppy growers rely heavily on their earnings from opium to purchase their daily necessities.

In traditional highland society, two corporate structures form the most important social institutions. The largest institution is the village, made up of houses mainly of the same ethnic group. However, in the villages of the opium poppy-growing groups, there may be one or more houses of traders who are "Haw" or Yunnanese Chinese, Shan, Lue or NorthernThai. There are also other ethnic persons who do seasonal work as wage earners for opium - producing households. These migrant workers are often paid in opium and are usually addicts who have chosen to take up residence in that village.

Villages of the same ethnic group are widely scattered and may be surrounded by villages of other ethnic groups (see the TRI map prepared for *Highlanders of Thailand*). Normally there is a main settlement with one or more small hamlets located in the general vicinity. Such hamlets form because there may be limited space in the original village, some people want to live closer to cultivable land, or some wish to live in a group consisting of only their own relatives.

Hill tribe villages are likely to break up at any time for many reasons, such as : shortage of good cropland nearby, dissatisfaction with village leaders, intravillage disputes, disputes with neighbouring villages, frequent harassment by bandits, many deaths in quick succession of either villagers or their livestock, expulsion of new religious converts by the traditional group, and,in more recent years, fear of terrorism by political insurgents. Dispersion is more frequent among the opium-poppy growing communities.

Highland villages, except those of the Lisu, are led by a headman with one or more assistants. This is especially likely if a village is formed by many households coming from different places. In general, the headman is responsible for maintaining the peace, settling disputes, hosting visitors to the village, and also acting as the village liaison with government authorities. In a mature village, there is usually an informal council of elders whose advice is sought on important issues by the headman. This council participates in the making of all important decisions which affect the village. Typical issues include whether the village should be moved to a new site or not, whether outsiders should be allowed to cut swiddens on village land, or whether a particular household should be expelled.

In tribal culture there is no supra - village organization. This also means there is no higher leader or chieftain for each tribe who can extend his power over all villages belonging to his ethnic group.

Most highlanders are animists and mostly pantheists who belive in spirits of all kinds: heavenly spirits, natural spirits, ancestral spirits, house spirits and spirits in certain things. These spirits, either benevolent or malevolent, usually require propitiation and sacrifice; and for some tribes, their highest and most respected spirits are godlike. Many cases of sickness are believed to be caused by offended spirits, especially the evil ones. These spirits are considered to have cast bad fortune on the individual or group concerned by taking away their souls, causing sickness, and harming their livestock. Either the shaman or the religious leader must diagnose the cause of sickness. The benevolent spirits are requested to come and are provided with offerings in return for force the evil ones to return the soul to the sick person. However,many spirits can be either benevolent or malevolent depending on whether or not they are treated properly.

In some tribes, the religious leaders also perform villagewide rituals and pray for the welfare and prosperity of the whole village or individual households. These people are therefore very important local leaders in highland society, and in some tribes, like the Pwo Karen, the shaman may also be the village headman. In traditional groups, with the exception of the Lua, most of whom are well integrated into lowland society, there are no social classes. The only group which might be defined as exclusive is that of the village elders who are widely respected beyond their own households. In other words, highland society is egalitarian.

The second important corporate structure in tribal villages is the household. Hill tribe households consist either of the extended or the nuclear family. The most prevalent type is the extended family household. The nuclear family household consists of just two generations, a husband and his wife and their children. Extended family housholds are more common among the Meo and the Yao. These people are also polygynous, while the Lahu, Lisu, Akha, Karen, Lua, H'tin and Khamu are monogamous.

The household is the basic socio-economic unit charged with the responsibility of providing food, shelter, welfare, education, religious training, and socialization.

KAREN

The Karen, or *Yang* as they are called by the Northern Thai, or *Kariang* as they are known to Thais in other parts of the country, are the largest highland group in Thailand. In 1995, the Karen population was estimated 321,900, which equalled 46.34 percent of the total hill tribe population of the country. Karen communities are located mainly in the mountainous areas of the western provinces along the Thai-Burmese border (**Chiang Rai, Chiang Mai, Mae Hong Son, Tak, Kanchanaburi and Phrachuap Khiri Khan**) and are scattered is some provinces in north and central Thailand (**Lampang, Lamphun, Sukhothai, Phrae, Kamphaeng Phet, Phetchaburi, Uthai Thani, Suphanburi and Ratchaburi**).Over the past 200 years they have tended to move eastward away from Burma into Thailand because of political conflicts with the Burmese.

The Karen belong to the Sino-Tibetan linguistic family. They are divided into four major sub groups:

1. The Skaw Karen or White Karen who call themselves and other subgroups Pga-gan-Yaw.

2. The Pwo Karen or Plong who are also known as White Karen but sometimes they are wrongly called Red Karen.

13

3. The Pa-O or Taungthu who are also known as Black Karen.

4. The Bwe or Kayah or Red Karen.

Karen settlements tend to be in areas of lower altitude compared with those of other tribes. Most of them are located in valleys or mountain saddles at an average height of 500 metres above sea level. Karen villages are sedentary and some villages have been established for more than a hundred years. Unlike other tribes, they have clearly recognised garden and village boundaries. Each village maintains its own sense of sovereignty and people from outside are not allowed to cultivate land within its territory unless they have rights over paddy fields gained either through purchase or inheritance.

Although many Karen construct terraced fields for wet rice, nearly all are also engaged in swidden cultivation. The shifting cultivation method of the Karen is called *land rotation or cyclical bush fallow*. Rice and vegetables are their major crops. Today some Karen may grow opium but it is not a traditional crop.

The Karen raise various kinds of domestic animals including pigs, chickens, water buffaloes, cattle and elephants. Some animals, mostly chickens, are killed for ceremonial offerings and feasts, and others are used as beasts of burden. The Karen derive cash income from the sale of cattle, and local produce,from wage labour, and by hiring out their elephants.

Karen kinship and marriage custom are different from those of other highlanders. Kinship is traced through the maternal line and residence is matrilocal. The Karen practise monogamy, and most households are nuclear. In all cases, the family represents the most important basic cooperative unit in all domestic affairs.

In Thailand, the Karen mostly practise the Buddhism and Animism. And some follow the Christian faith. Their New Year celebration takes place in January or February.

HMONG

The Hmong or Mong are called Meo in Thai. This ethnic group, like the Yao, belongs to the Meo-Yao branch of the Austro-Thai linguistic family.

The Hmong are one of the most spread out minority groups. They are scattered throughout South China in Kweichow, Hunan, Szechwan, Kwangxi, and Yunnan provinces. There are also Hmong communities in North Vietnam, Laos, Thailand and even a few in Burma. In Thailand, the number of Hmong people in 1995 was approximately 124,211 the second largest group after the Karen and made up 17.88 percent of all tribesmen in the country. The Meo settlement is concentrated in thirteen provinces : **Chiang Mai, Chiang Rai, Nan, Phrae, Tak, Lampang, Phayao, Phetchabun, Kamphaeng Phet, Mae Hong Son, Sukhothai, Pitsanulok and Loei.** Three subgroups of Meo are found in Thailand:

1. The Blue Hmong (Mong Njua), who are also known as the black Meo, Flowery Meo or Striped Meo in Thai. Women in the subgroup wear the distinctive indigo-dyed pleated skirt or kilt with a batik design.

2. The White Hmong (Hmong Daw). White Hmong women wear a white pleated skirt only on ceremonial occasions, but when engaged in everyday work, they put on indigo-dyed trousers.

16

Pwo Karen

Kayah woman

Karen at work

Hmong woman with needle work

Hmong Women

Hmong Men

Lahu Women

Lahu playing music

Lahu New Year festival

3. The last subgroup is known as the Gua M'ba Meo (Hmong Gua M'ba) which literary means Arm-band Hmong and only recently entered Thailand from Laos. They are actually a subgroup of the White Hmong. Most are confined to refugee camps.

The extended Hmong family is patrilineal, and polygyny is allowed. The family is the most important basic unit of social organization. Beyond the family level, the clan serves as the centre for all activities that mark the uniqueness and unity of the Hmong people. The available information indicates that there are eleven clans in Thailand. The names and origins of these clans are recited in Hmong legends.

Hmong religion is a combination of pantheism and shamanism with the emphasis on ancestor-worship. The Chinese influence is obvious in their beliefs and practices.

The Hmong prefer to locate their villages at high altitudes (1,000-1,200 m.). They are pioneer or primary - shifting cultivators. Rice and corn are the main subsistence crops, and opium is the principal cash crop. The Hmong are more heavily engaged in opium production than any other highlanders in Thailand.

The New Year celebration which normally takes place in December is the most important festivity.

LAHU

The Lahu,or Musur as the Shan and the Thai call them, also belong to the Tibeto-Burman branch of the Sino-Tibetan linguistic family. It is believed that they originated in the Tibetan Plateau and over the centuries migrated to China, Burma, Laos and Thailand.

In Thailand, Lahu are found in five povinces: **Chiang Rai, Chiang Mai, Mae Hong Son,Tak and Kamphaeng Phet.** In 1995 there were approximately 73,252 which equalled 10.54 percent of the total hill tribe population.

The Lahu are divided into several ethnic subgroups of which only six are present in Thailand. These are:

1. Lahu Nyi or Musur Daeng
2. Lahu Na or Musur Dam
3. Lahu Shehleh or Musur Na Muey
4. Lahu Laba
5. Lahu Phu
6. Lahu Shi

These main subgroups are further subdivided into smaller groups.

Lahu villages are usually located high in the mountains at about 1,000 metres. When they establish their communities at some distance from a source of water they build a series of bamboo pipes to bring water into the village.

Lahu society is cognatic and monogamous. The nuclear family forms the most common domestic unit and plays the most important part in the social and political organization of the village. When a Lahu man marries a woman from another village, he is expected to live with his parents-in-law (uxorilocally) for a certain time to provide bride-service. In such cases, the household becomes extended but usually for not more than 5 - 6 years. Kinship ties are not particularly important in the Lahu society. However, it is possible for political leaders to gain high acceptance and respect.

The Lahu base their economy primarily on swidden agriculture. Like other pioneer swiddeners, the Lahu clear fields in the forest by slash-and-burn. A plot of land is used for as long as the yields are good, and after the soil becomes exhausted,the owner looks for other places to exploit.

Today, the Lahu staple crops are dry rice and corn. Many varieties of cash crops are also grown e.g. melons, peppers, beans, yams, millet, and vegetables. In some villages, opium remains an important cash crop. Animal husbandry is also important, and every household raises pigs, fowl, cattle and horses for various purposes such as for feasts, and ceremonial offerings and for transport.

The Lahu are theistic animists ruled by one god named *Geusha*. Like their highland neighbours, they also worship their ancestors. In Burma, the Lahu were considerably influenced by Buddhism and Christianity. A large number become Christian during and immediately following British rule.Most Lahu in Thailand follow their old beliefs. Religious practitioners remain prominent in Lahu society. The New Year ceremony (Kho Cha Lor), the most important event, is held for five days between January and March to thank their god *Geusha*.

YAO

The Yao or Mien as they call themselves, are linguistically grouped together with the Meo tribe in the Meo-Yao branch of the Austro-Thai family.

The Yao can be found in Kwangxi and Kwangtung Provinces of South China, in Vietnam, Laos, Burma, and North Thailand. In Thailand, the number of Yao in 1995 was estimated at 40,371 and made up 5.81 percent to the total hill tribe population. The major concentration of Yao residents are found in **Chiang Rai, Phayao and Nan Province.** Nevertheless, there are also a few Yao villages in **Chiang Mai, Lampang, Sukhothai, Kamphaeng Phet, and Tak.**

Although the Yao grow opium, the cultivation of dry rice and corn is more important to them.

Households with extended families are common, and polygamous marriage is practised. Like the Hmong, Mien boys must choose their wives from outside their clans. When a proper bride price is paid they take thier wives to live with their parents and any children automatically become members of the father's patrilineal clan. If a man is poor or a woman is an only daughter, the man may decide to live uxorilocally. He may either live all his life with his wife's family or live with them for just a few years before taking his family back to his parental house. Premarital sexual relationships are common and cross-cousin marriage is preferred. The adoption of children from outside or inside the tribe is widely practised.

Perhaps more than any other tribes, the Yao have adopted many characteristics of Chinese culture. They use Chinese characters to record traditional songs, migratory histories, legends, and the names of ancestors. They also hold their New Year celebration on the same days as the Chinese. The Yao are regarded as pantheists and ancestor-worshippers, and the influence of the popular Toism is evident.

Yao in marriage costume

Yao at ceremony

Yao House

Akha woman

Akha village gate

Akha Swinging Festival

Lisu woman

Lisu men

Lisu New Year Festival

AKHA

The Akha call themselves A-Kha whereas the Thai people refer to them as Kaw or E-kaw. They are historically linked with the ancient Lolo tribes that inhabit South Yunnan. The Akha belong to the Tibeto-Burman branch of the Sino-Tibetan linguistic family.

It is generally believed that the Akha originated in the Tibetan Highlands. Over the years they left their homeland and migrated south to Yunnan, North Burma, Laos, and North Thailand.

It is not known when the first Akha settlement was established on Thai soil, but it is thought that this took place in the 1800's.

Most of the Akha in Thailand prefer to live along mountain ridges at an altitude of approximately 1,000 m. In the past, their settlements were limited mainly to the north bank of the Mae Kok river, and they rarely moved south. In more recent times, as a result of population pressure,the Akha began to spread out of the Mae Kok basin in search of better land. Today,Akha are found in six provinces : **Chiang Rai, Chiang Mai, Tak, Kamphang Phet, Lampang and Phrae.** Due to the lack of data, the exact number of Akha living in Thailand is not known. However the 1995 statistics indicate that the population is in excess of 48,468 spread over 258 villages. Newcomers from Burma are constantly arriving.

The salient social unit is the extended family. Patrilineal clans mediate all relationships concerning kinship ties, marriage, residential patterns, and rights of succession. The Akha are customarily monogamous. In practice, however, there is no rule which prohibits an Akha man from having more than one wife. After marriage, Akha men live patrilocally.

The Akha are shifting cultivators. They cultivate dry rice for consumption and grow corn, millet, peppers, beans, garlic, sesame and other varieties of vegetables as additional subsistence crops.Crop production is often inadequate to meet their needs. Domestic animals, including fowl, pigs and water buffaloes are also raised by the Akha for special feasts and sacrifices.

The Akha are pantheists who place special emphasis upon ancestor-worship and spirit offerings.

The four day *Swinging ceremony*, the most enjoyable ceremonial event, is held during mid-August to mid-September. The Akha celebrate their New Year in December for four days. Those who want to draw the Akha into closer affiliation with lowland civilization often see their complex rituals as being a major obstacle to modernization. Akha society is under extreme pressure to change and partly as a consequence of this, the incidence of opium addiction is high.

LISU

The Lisu,or Lisaw as they are called by Thais, inhabit the mountainous hinterland of North Thailand. According to the 1995 survey, the number of Lisu in Thailand was 27,899 which totalled 4.02 percent of the total hill tribe population. Today Lisu are found living scattered throughout the nine northern povinces : **Chiang Mai, Chiang Rai, Phayao, Mae Hong Son, Tak, Lampang, Sukhothai, Kamphaeng Phet, and Phetchabun.**

The Lisu are believed to have originated in southern China and first appeared in Chiang Rai Province about 80 years ago. The Lisu belong to the Tibeto-Burman branch of the Sino-Tibetan linguistic family. They are divided into two ethnic subgroups:
1. The Flowery or Hua Lisu
2. The Black or He Lisu.

Most of the Lisu in Thailand are flowery Lisu.

Lisu settlements are located in the highlsnds at an average altitude of about 1,000 metres.Like most hill people, the Lisu are heavily engaged in agriculture.

They grow rice, corn, and vegetables as subsistence crops and grow opium for sale. They draw additional income from the sale of domesticated animals such as pigs and cattle.

The Lisu tribe is made up of several patrilineal clans. The clan is important because it stands as the chief determinant of kinship relations and marriage rules. Monogamy and clan exogamy are the ideal practices which, when followed, strengthen familial ties and provide a cohesive force in Lisu society. Kinship relations are centred on the family and extended in increasingly wider circles to the tribe as a whole. Lisu solidarity, despite the lack of a political secular leader at village level, depends on this in a way that differentiates them from other tribes.

Culturally speaking,the Lisu have adopted much which is Chinese. For example, they celebrate their New Year on the same day as the Chinese. They are, however, principally animists and ancestor-worshippers and their reputation as individualists makes them quite distinct.

LAWA

The Lawa or Lua as the northern Thai call them, are found only in Thailand. The Lawa identify themselves as Lavu'a (La-woe-a). It is estimated that the Lawa people, once known as the Milakkha or Lowa, migrated into the northern region of the Mae Ping valley around 660 A.D. They are of Austro-Asiatic stock and according to protohistorical tradition,they are believed to be the first settlers in North Thailand. They are linguistically closely related to the Mon-Khmer and have largely been absorbed into Thai society.

In 1995 those who retained a seperate identity in the highlands numbered 15,711 and made up 2.26 percent of the tribal population. Most were found to be living on the Bo Luang plateau southwest of **Chiang Mai** and in the mountainous area of Umpai, southeast of **Mae Hong Son.**

The Lawa practise shiffing cultivation of the rotational type and are skillful in making wet rice terraces. They are recognised as being the most conservation - minded land users in the highlands.

36

The Lawa society is similar to that of other tribes in that descent is traced patrilineally and marriage is monogamous. Their society is regarded as having a dual structure. Most members are classified as Lua or common people. A small group who trace descent from Khun Luang Wilanka, a proto-historical Lua King, are called Kun.

The Lawa are animists and ancestor- worshippers who,like the Thai, combine their traditional beliefs with Buddhism.

KHAMU

The Khamu are one of the smallest tribal groups living in Northern Thailand, principally along the Thai-Laotian border of Nan Province. They belong to the Mon-Khmer branch of the Austro-Asiatic linguistic family. In 1995 they numbered 10,153 and equalled only 1.46 percent of the total hill tribe population.

Most of the Khamu in Thailand come from Luang Prabang, Xieng Khoung and Vientiane in Laos. In Thailand, most of Khamu are concentrated in Nan Province and still make their livings in the mountains. They first migrated into the country as labourers and worked either in the teak forests or in similarly isolated places. At the end of their contracts, they decided to settle rather than return to their native villages in Laos. Besides **Nan**, they are also found in **Lampang** and **Kanchanaburi** Provinces.

The Khamu trace descent patrilineally and traditionally adhere to the custom of patrilocal residence. They live in small villages located on mountain slopes and survive on subsistence agriculture supplemented by hunting, fishing and trading.

The Khamu practise an animistic religion. In Laos, Khamu shamans are considered to be excellent magic-religious practitioners and are often invited to participate in Laotian ceremonies.

Lawa house

Lawa woman

Khamu women

H'tin women

Mlabri Men

Mlabri house

Padaung Woman

Padaung in full dress

H'TIN

The H'tin are migratory swidden farmers in the northern Laos-Thailand border area. They are called Tin, Thin, or Kha T'in by Thais. In Laos, they are called Phai or Kha Phai. However,in Thailand, they call themselves "Mal" or "Prai". This ethic group is also classified as belonging to the Mon-Khmer branch of the Austro-Asiatic linguistic family.

From available reports it appears that the H'tin have lived in Thailand for a very long time. In 1995 they numbered 32,755 which equalled 4.71 percent of the total hill tribe population. All of their villages are found in Nan Province. They live in houses built on piles with bamboo floors and walls. They practise swidden agriculture and grow glutinous rice, the staple rice, variety of Northern Thai lowlanders.

The H'tin are monogamous. After marriage, residence is initially matrilocal, in the house of the wife's parents. After the birth of several children, the couple normally move to a new dwelling.

Except for those who live near the lowland Thai and have become Buddhists, the H'tin are animists. Some H'tin villages have the Buddhist temples.

MLABRI

The Mlabri or Yumbri, known to the Thai as the P'hi Tong Luang or *Spirits of the Yellow Leaves,* are also known to the Hmong as Ma Ku. These people are dispersed in extremely small, highly nomadic, family bands. Some linguists place the Mlabri language in an eastern subgroup of Palaung-Wa, together with Khamu and Lamet. However, recent research indicates that the Mlabri language is Austro-Asiatic and closely related to Mon-Khmer.

Although in the past,the Mlabri lived in **Chiang Mai**, **Chiang Rai**, and **Kengtung in Burma,** only a few can now be found in **Nan** and **Phrae Provinces.** According to 1995 survey the total population in Thailand is around 182 persons.

These people used to rely almost exclusively on hunting and gathering. By custom they cannot own rice fields but they can work as labourers in the fields of others such as the Hmong and the Thai. They used to move their campsites every three or four days depending on the availability of their natural food supply.

The Mlabri practise patrilineal descent and live in nuclear families. The basic unit to their social organization is the band, consisting of three to a dozen members.

PADAUNG

The Padaung, well-known as the people with long necks or the giraffe-necked women, are a sub-group of Karen(Bwe Group) living in Kayah state of Eastern Burma bodering Northern Thailand. The population numbered about 30,000 in 1978. They call themselves "Lae Kur" or "Kayan". Their language is one of the Kenmic group in the Tibeto-Burman language family. In Thailand, only a few families of Padaung have settled temporarily as refugees in **Muang** District of **Mae Hong Son Province.**

The greatest attraction of Padaung culture is the extraodinary jewellery still worn by most of women. They usually wear a row of brass rings that do not actually stretch their necks but in fact squash the vertebrae and collar bones. It is said that a woman generally has about twenty or more rings around her neck. In addition, over the collar they wear beads and necklaces made of silver chains and coins.

According to their traditions, a special ceremony is performed for a woman at 5-10 years of age when she puts on the first five rings. The other rings are added in the later years.They wear the rings not only for decoration and beauty but also because of their beliefs.   The Padaung myth states that a long time ago,   the spirits were angered with the people and sent a plague of tigers to eat the women. For fear of the women being killed, the ancestors suggested that all of them wear the brass rings to protect themselves.

The Padaung cultivate both dry rice and wet rice.   Rice is their main crop, and they grow it using both slash-and-burn cultivation and buffalo ploughing.

Most of Padaung are animists, but about 10 percent are Buddhists. Now, the number of Christians is increasing because of the Roman Catholic   mission   in   the area for more than 100 years. The annual festival for the fertility and prosperity of the whole community is usually held at the beginning of the rainy season.   Sacrifices are made to the spirits for good health and bountiful harvests.

— — — — — — — — —

References

1. Forsyth, Tim. "Refugees and freaks: Plight of the Long Neck people" **Bangkok Post** Vol. XLVI No. 313, 1991. p. 21.

2. **Illustrated Encyclopedia of Mankind,** Vl.12, London, Marshall Cavendish Limited, 1978. p. 1549-1551.

3. Somsong Burutpat.   "Padaung:Long Neck Karen" **Journal of Language and Culture,** Vol.8 No.2 Mahidol University, 1989. P.24-37

PROVINCES WITH HILL TRIBE SETTLEMENTS

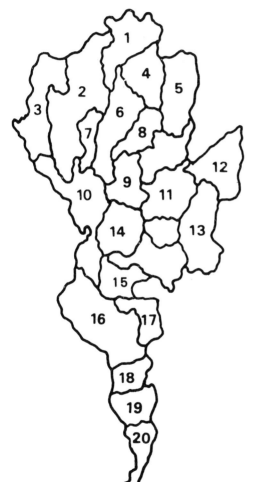

1. Chiang Rai
2. Chiang Mai
3. Mae Hong Son
4. Phayao
5. Nan
6. Lampang
7. Lamphun
8. Phrae
9. Sukhothai
10. Tak
11. Phitsanulok
12. Loei
13. Phetchabun
14. Kamphaeng Phet
15. Uthai Thani
16. Kanchanaburi
17. Suphun Buri
18. Ratchaburi
19. Phetchaburi
20. Prachuab Khiri Khan

HILL TRIBE
SETTLEMENTS

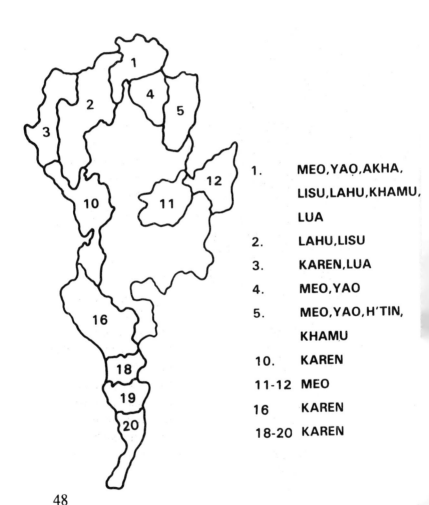

1. MEO,YAO,AKHA,
  LISU,LAHU,KHAMU,
  LUA

2. LAHU,LISU

3. KAREN,LUA

4. MEO,YAO

5. MEO,YAO,H'TIN,
  KHAMU

10. KAREN

11-12 MEO

16 KAREN

18-20 KAREN

CLASSIFICATION OF HILL TRIBES
BY AGRICULTURAL PRACTICE

OPIUM -POPPY GROWING TRIBES	(TRADITIONALLY) NON OPIUM -POPPY GROWING TRIBES
MEO, YAO, LAHU, AKHA, LISU	KAREN, LUA, H'TIN, KHAMU
LAND USE : Primary Forest Cultivation, Shifting-Cultivation	LAND USE Secondary Forest Cultivation, Cyclical Bush Fallow Cultivation, Land Rotation
RESULT : Quick Soil Exhaustion, Migration	RESULT : More Stabilized Residence

FARM CALENDAR OF OPIUM-POPPY GROWING TRIBES

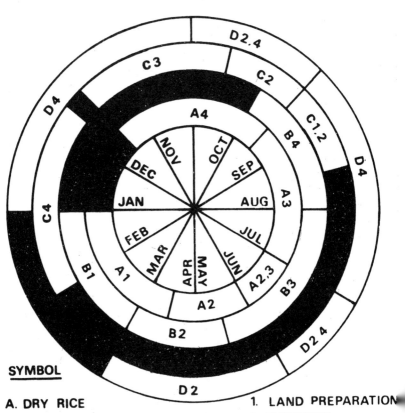

SYMBOL

A. DRY RICE
B. MAIZE
C. OPIUM-POPPY
D. OTHER CROPS

1. LAND PREPARATION
2. GROWING
3. WEEDING
4. HARVESTING

50

FARM CALENDAR OF NON OPIUM-POPPY GROWING TRIBES

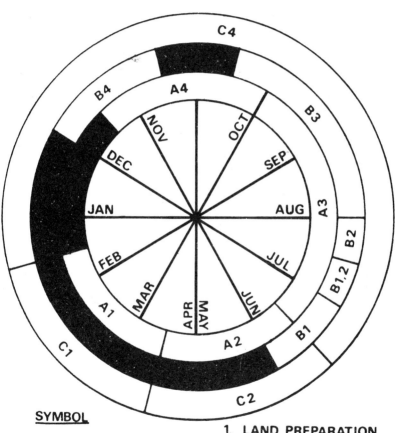

SYMBOL

A. DRY RICE
B. PADDY RICE
C. OTHER CROPS

1. LAND PREPARATION
2. GROWING
3. WEEDING
4. HARVESTING

51

Traditional Socio-Agricultural Calendar of the Hill Tribes in Thailand

Months / Tribes	January	February	March	April	May	June	July	August	September	October	November	December
Karen	Village ceremony	Site selection	Slashing	Field burning	Rice planting	Feild Spirit offerring	Paddy field spirit offering	Weeding	Rat Trapping	Early rice harvesting	Yearly rice harvesting	Rice threshing
Meo	New Year festival	Opium-poppy incising	Field clearing	Field burning	Rice planting	Weeding	Weeding	Weeding	Poppy seed sowing	Thinning opium field	Rice harvesting	New Year festival
Yao	Embroi-dering	Ceremo-nies held	Field clearing	Field burning	Rice, maize planting	Weeding	Weeding	Multiple crops hasvesting	Poppy seed sowing	Early rice harvesting	Yearly rice harvesting	Rice threshing
Akha	Weaving	Field clearing	Field burning	Calling rice soul ceremony	Rice planting	Weeding	Weeding	Swinging ceremony	Maize harvesting	Early rice harvesting	Yearly rice harvesting	New Year festival
Lisu	First New Year festival	Second New Year festival	Field clearing	Field burning	Rice dibbling	Weeding	Weeding	Soul calling ceremony	Maize harvesting	Poppy seed sowing	Rice harvesting	Rice threshing

Months / Tribes	January	February	March	April	May	June	July	August	September	October	November	December
Lahu	Scoring poppy pods	New Year festival	Field burning	Field spirit house setting	Rice planting	Weeding	Weeding	Weeding	House spirit ceremony	Opium field spirit ceremony	Rice harvesting and rice soul calling ceremony	Village spirit offering
Lua	Ancestor spirit ceremony	Forest spirit offering and site selection	Field preparing	New Year festival	Ploughing	Paddy field	Weeding	Multiple crops harvesting	Early rice harvesting	Early rice harvesting	Yearly rice harvesting	Village spirit offering
H'tin	Site selection	Field spirit offering	Cutting and falling the trees	New Year festival	Rice dibbling	Weeding	Weeding	Multiple crops harvesting	Early rice harvesting	Early rice harvesting	Yearly rice harvesting	New Year festival
Khamu	New Year festival	Cutting and falling the trees	Field burning	Ceremony to ensure good fortune	Rice dibbling	Weeding	Weeding	Field spirit offering	Early rice harvesting	Early rice harvesting	Yearly rice harvesting	Rice threshing

TRIBAL POPULATION SUMMARY IN THAILAND

PROVINCE NAME		ETHNIC GROUPS									TOTAL
		KAREN	MEO	LAHU	LISU	YAO	AKHA	LUA	HTIN	KHAMU	
Chiang Mai	*	728	61	153	56	6	20	25	-	-	1,049
	**	19,723	2,112	5,316	1,978	265	557	1,814	-	-	31,765
	***	106,116	17,198	27,392	10,873	1,145	2,609	8,862	-	-	174,195
Chiang Rai	*	39	45	223	49	60	229	9	-	7	661
	**	1,303	2,881	6,198	1,466	1,806	7,117	233	-	338	21,342
	***	6,375	20,099	34,091	9,121	13,592	43,438	1,676	-	1,971	130,363
Kamphaengphet	*	6	7	3	2	12	-	-	-	-	30
	**	212	412	155	43	442	-	-	-	-	1,264
	***	1,086	3,136	804	229	3,231	-	-	-	-	8,556
Kanchanaburi	*	138	-	-	-	-	-	-	-	-	138
	**	3,534	-	-	-	-	-	-	-	-	3,534
	***	18,358	-	-	-	-	-	-	-	-	18,358

PROVINCE NAME		ETHNIC GROUPS									TOTAL
		KAREN	MEO	LAHU	LISU	YAO	AKHA	LUA	H'TIN	KHAMU	
Lampang	*	21	7	5	1	21	6	-	-	1	62
	**	729	131	83	20	734	149	12	-	25	1,883
	***	3,613	935	716	118	4,943	909	69	-	132	11,435
Lamphun	*	64	-	-	-	-	-	-	-	-	64
	**	4,980	-	-	-	-	-	-	-	-	4,980
	***	23,645	-	-	-	-	-	-	-	-	23,645
Loei	*	-	1	-	-	-	-	-	-	-	1
	**	-	90	-	-	-	-	-	-	-	90
	***	-	616	-	-	-	-	-	-	-	616
Mae Hong Son	*	479	13	28	18	-	-	16	-	-	554
	**	14,501	267	876	906	-	-	797	-	-	17,347
	***	76,632	2,740	5,147	5,065	-	-	4,763	-	-	94,347

PROVINCE NAME		ETHNIC GROUPS									TOTAL
		KAREN	MEO	LAHU	LISU	YAO	AKHA	LUA	H'TIN	KHAMU	
Nan	*	-	25	1	-	36	-	-	147	21	230
	**	-	2,081	8	-	966	-	-	6,088	1,551	10,694
	***	-	16,809	44	-	8,370	-	-	32,745	7,705	65,673
Phayao	*	-	9	-	1	31	-	-	-	-	41
	**	-	737	-	33	1,126	-	-	-	-	1,896
	***	-	5,918	-	184	7,796	-	-	-	-	13,898
Phrae	*	14	4	-	1	-	2	-	-	-	21
	**	1,855	199	-	8	-	63	-	-	-	2,125
	***	8,160	1,928	-	62	-	333	-	-	-	10,483
Phitsanulok	*	2	10	-	-	-	-	-	-	-	12
	**	130	794	-	-	-	-	-	-	-	924
	***	687	5,430	-	-	-	-	-	-	-	6,117

PROVINCE NAME	ETHNIC GROUPS										TOTAL
	KAREN	MEO	LAHU	LISU	YAO	AKHA	LUA	HTIN	KHAMU		
Phetchabun *	-	18	1	1	1	-	-	1	-		22
Phetchabun **	-	3,590	3	118	15	-	-	2	-		3,728
Phetchabun ***	-	28,281	8	800	83	-	-	10	-		29,182
Phetchaburi *	26	-	-	-	-	-	-	-	-		26
Phetchaburi **	581	-	-	-	-	-	-	-	-		581
Phetchaburi ***	3,003	-	-	-	-	-	-	-	-		3,003
Prachuap Khiri Khan *	5	-	-	-	-	-	-	-	-		5
Prachuap Khiri Khan **	148	-	-	-	-	-	-	-	-		148
Prachuap Khiri Khan ***	748	-	-	-	-	-	-	-	-		748
Ratchaburi *	46	-	-	-	-	-	-	-	-		46
Ratchaburi **	1,242	-	-	-	-	-	-	-	-		1,242
Ratchaburi ***	5,849	-	-	-	-	-	-	-	-		5,849

PROVINCE NAME		ETHNIC GROUPS									TOTAL
		KAREN	MEO	LAHU	LISU	YAO	AKHA	LUA	HTIN	KHAMU	
Sukhothai	*	-	-	-	2	5	-	-	-	-	7
	**	-	-	-	31	107	-	-	-	-	138
	***	-	-	-	174	802	-	-	-	-	976
Suphan Buri	*	9	-	-	-	-	-	-	-	-	9
	**	610	-	-	-	-	-	-	-	-	610
	***	2,796	-	-	-	-	-	-	-	-	2,796
Tak	*	425	43	7	4	1	1	-	-	-	481
	**	11,578	2,825	668	199	64	164	-	-	-	15,525
	***	61,226	21,121	5,050	1,203	409	1,179	-	-	-	90,188
Uthai Thani	*	34	-	-	-	-	-	3	-	3	40
	**	680	-	-	-	-	-	67	-	74	821
	***	3,606	-	-	-	-	-	341	-	345	4,292

PROVINCE NAME	ETHNIC GROUPS										TOTAL
	KAREN	MEO	LAHU	LISU	YAO	AKHA	LUA	H'TIN	KHAMU		
Tot. Villages	2,132	243	421	135	173	258	53	148	32		3,595
Tot. H/Holds	60,385	16,146	13,307	4,802	5,525	8,050	2,923	6,090	1,988		119,216
Tot./Persons	321,900	124,211	73,252	27,899	40,371	48,468	15,711	32,755	10,153		694,720
Percentage	46.34	17.88	10.54	4.02	5.81	6.98	2.26	4.71	1.46		100

Note   *   No. of Villages

       **   No. of Household

       ***   No. of Persons

1   The total number of population in Chiang Mai Province exclude the **Palong** who just migrated to Thailand with 4 Villages, 90 househlds and 485 persons.

2   The total number of population in Nan Province exclude 125 persons of the Mlabri.

3   The total number of population in Phrae province exclude 7 households and 57 persons of the Mlabri.

Source :   Service and Publicity Section

           Tribal Research Institute

           Chiang Mai 50200 Thailand

SOME SOUND ADVICE
FOR HILL TRIBE TREKKERS

A great number of the tourists visiting Chiang Mai make enquiries about hilltribe trekking. They come looking for adventure and a learning experience that will last a life-time. The experience of a trek around the Chiang Mai area usually includes beautiful mountain terrain,wild jungles, clean rivers, photogenic waterfalls and unusually shaped caves. The visitors can journey to these places by foot, by horseback or on the back of an elephant. Travelling by longtail boats and jeeps is also becoming more and more popular as tour agencies expand their approach to trekking.

The Tourist Authority of Thailand wants to help visitors seeking information about trekking agencies. Here is a list of some guidelines for potential trekkers to follow.

1. Before going on a trek, it is a good idea to familiarize yourself with the different hilltribes and their cultures. A good place to start is to visit the *Tribal Research Institute* located on the campus of Chiang Mai University. The Institute has a very informative museum about each of the hilltribes. The exhibits include costumes worn by the different tribes, maps and charts telling about hilltribe festivals and each tribes farming cycle. There is also a very

informative library containing up-to-date books about each hill tribe group. The Tribal Research Institute is open weekdays from 8.30-16.30. For slide and film shows as well as a short brief on the hill tribes, visiting groups are suggested to inform the Institute in advance.

2. TAT Chiang Mai does not have any organized trekking tours but will gladly hand out an information sheet with a list of the private companies specializing in trekking tours. Read this sheet and then do some shopping around.

3. Some of the better companies specializing in trekking tours are members of local trekking clubs. The guides are usually licensed and have studied at a school which offers training in the tourist industry. It is recommended that you take advantage of their expertise. They know the trekking areas very well and often can speak the hill tribe languages. Their English is quite good and so is their knowledge of hill tribe culture. It is always a good idea to speak with your guide beforehand to check their language skills.

4. All treks must be registered with the Tourist Police before departure. This is done for your protection. Companies which don't adhere to this are breaking the law and putting you in a potentially dangerous situation. You should avoid these companies.

5. Recently, some trekking companies and guides have used narcotics to lure tourists. Some

have even asked hill tribes to demonstrate the use of narcotics. These tactics, when used, are detrimental and can get you in trouble. Remember that in Thailand, there are laws with stiff penalties concerning the use of narcotics. All visitors are welcome to make enquiries with the Tourist Police to find out which companies have a bad reputation with the police department.

6. Keep your valuables, such as your passport, jewellery and money, in a safe at your hotel or guest house while trekking upcountry.

7. Protect yourself against the nasty little mosquitoes of Northern Thailand, but don't rely on the use of prophylactic drugs. In Thailand, the many different strains of malaria parasites are resistant to many of the drugs on the market. You should protect yourself by wearing long pants, long-sleeved shirts, thick socks and a scarf around your neck. While trekking, also use a strong band of mosquito repellent. At night you should sleep under a mosquito net and avoid outdoor activities between dusk and dawn when malaria-carrying mosquitoes are out. For additional information about malaria you can call (053) 221529 and talk to someone at the Malaria Centre of Chiang Mai.

8. TAT Chiang Mai has long realized the importance of the varied hill tribes in Thailand and has tried to help preserve and promote the hill tribes cultures and traditions. Information about the culture

and way of life of each tribe is shared among government agencies, trekking tour companies, guesthouse owners, the media and tourists themselves. As a visitor you should remember :

8.1 Respect hill tribe beliefs and religious symbols and structures. Be careful about what you touch. It is better to ask your guide about some do's and don'ts before entering a hill tribe village.

8.2 Dress appropriately. Hill tribe people are generally modest and it may offend them if you stroll around in skimpy clothings.

8.3 Ask before taking a photograph of someone. Some villages do not even permit being photographed.

8.4 Avoid trading western medicines and articles of clothing. Many of the hill tribe people are not familiar with the use of western medicines. And by trading clothing, you may add a new style of dressing and grooming contrary to their own. If you want to give something, it should be something to contribute to their welfare. (pens, paper, needles, thread,cloth and material used for various hill tribe handicrafts, etc.)

9 Prices of treks are determined by the duration of the trek and the transportation used. The kind of meals available and the size of the trekking group will also affect the price.

(*Source* : Tourism Authority of Thailand. "Travel North" Vol.1 No. 3 Chiang Mai, 1989, p. 6-7)

HILL TRIBE PROBLEM

The problems stated in the national policy on the hill tribe during the past 30 years are:
1) Depletion of natural resources and environment
2) Opium cultivation
3) Security problems
4) Low standard of living

During the past 3 decades, the governmental, NGO's, and other volunteer organizations (especially the Royal Project) have helped solve the hill tribe problem. The situation is now much improved. However, new problems have arisen unexpectedly. Such problems resulted from people's ignorance, selfishness, and social changes.

1) **Deforestation in the highlands**
Deforestation is still going on though it has now lessened. The Land Sat 5 picture showed that in 1985 there was 49.59% forest cover in the northern part of Thailand where there mostly hill tribe people live. The highland development projects have been encouraging the tribal people to practise conservation farming while the people themselves are turning to sustainable farming (rice fields and fruit trees).

New problems started after development came to the highlands. Tourism increased and lowlanders became interested in buying land in the hills. Another problem is the over-use of pesticides in the hills which can cause serious danger to uplanders and lowlanders alike.

2) Opium cultivation

The Thai Government was successful in reducing the amount of opium produced in Thailand from 145 tons in 1967 to 24 tons in 1988. However, when less opium is available, it is imported from other countries and sold to these tribal people who are addicted. Besides, other kinds of drugs, such as heroin and stimulatants are now found in tribal villages.

3) National Security

In 1967, the Communist party was quite strong in some parts of Thailand. However, the government was able to control the situation by 1983 and was successful in turning the tribal activists into "cooperators with national development". Nevertheless, this matter of security is something we have to keep a watchful eye on so as to prevent the conflict with the minority.

4) Low standard of living among the hill tribes

Many positive changes are happening among

the hill tribes i.e. more hill tribe students are graduating from universities, hill tribe people are more familiar with modern medications, health care, and family planning; hill tribe people now earn more and grow more kinds of crops; and more hill tribe people are working outside their farms. However, new problems are also developing. More educated hill tribe people are unemployed; malnutrition occurs among some tribal children; and venereal disease and AIDS are increasingly found among the tribal people. Social changes and poverty are forcing people to come down to towns where they become labourers, beggars, or prostitutes. Tribal people are discarding their customs and traditional practises out of ignorance and a feeling that the old ways are not worth preserving. (for instance, the dances and herbal medications are disappearing).

The migration of members of their ethnic groups from neighbouring countries is another problem which is not yet solved.

Lisu house

Elephant riding

Yao woman

Lisu preparing offerring

Tourists at guest house

Karen playing music

Vegetable field

Paddy field

Lisu in the cold season

HILL TRIBE POLICY

There are 3 different approaches regarding the minorities : separation or segregation, assimilation, and integration. The Thai government is using the integration approach.

The Ministry of Interior Policy (1955) did not use the word "hill tribe" but "remote people" (Welfare for Remote People Policy). On June 3, 1959, the Hill Tribe Welfare Committee was first appointed. It was then when the National policy on the hill tribes started.

In 1959,the Department of Public Welfare was appointed to take responsibility for working with the hill tribes, together with the provincial hill tribe welfare committees. (with the Governor as Chairman). The policy dealt with the 4 major problems and did not concentrate on one particular case.

In 1982, the Premier Prem Tinsulanond was aware of the ineffeciency of the official work regarding the hill tribe problems and opium cultivation, so he had another committee appointed. The security and

opium issues were reviewed. The 1982 National Policy on the Hill Tribes (the security and opium issue) consisted of 3 aspects:
- Administration
- Opium and addiction
- Social and economic development

The work was to be undertaken at 3 different levels:

The National Level: composed of the National Security Committee on the Hill Tribes and opium growing.The Deputy Prime Minister as Chairman and the National Security Council Secretariat as a committee member and Secretary.

The Ministrial Level: composed of a central committee with the Minister of Interior as Chairman and the Director General of Department of Public Welfare as Secretary.

The Provincial Level : Provincial Hill tribe Committee.

In 1987 the Third Army stepped in and worked on the hill tribe problem as another regional organization working in cooperation with the national and provincial organizations. The Third Army has been appointed to work on specific missions such as hill tribe censuses, land use and housing.

In 1989 the National Policy on the hill tribes still effective today (1995) was laid down. It covers three aspects :

1. Political and administrative aspect

(1) Censuses be taken and Thai nationality be considered or granted to those who meet the qualifications. For those who are not granted Thai nationality, their certain legal status be stated in accordance with the regulation.

(2) Administration and management within hill tribe communities be organized in accordance with the law, with suitable working steps according to the people's readiness. For the communities in which systematic administration is not yet possible, suitable management procedures have to be developed so as to prepare the people for future democratic administration.

(3) Land and permanent residences be provided to the hill tribes. In doing this, however, certain matters must be taken into account, namely, local factors, socio-economic development, security and natural resource conservation.

(4) Official law and regulations be effective in every area,with strict punishment for those who break the law. Propaganda and appropriate pressure be posed so as to encourage the target people to obey the law.

(5) The hill tribes should have a correct

understanding of Thai society, of their rights and duties as Thai citizens under Thai law. This can be achieved through public relations work.

(6) Persistent actions be taken to prevent more immigrants from coming in and to force out the new migrants. Measures be set out to pressure those who draw immigrants, give them shelter, or facilitate hill tribe immigration.

(7) The influence of other minority groups and the Communist Party of Thailand be lessened by increasing the official staff efficiency in protecting and providing security for the hill tribes. The hill tribes should be able to protect themselves and become self-reliant to some degree.

2. Economic and Social Development

2.1 Uplifting the quality of life and income levels.

(1) Economic and social development of tribal society should be undertaken, stressing self-sufficience and natural resource preservation. Development should be done with regard to the situation. Availability of land and natural resources in the highlands should first be taken into consideration when permanent settlement is proposed to the people.

(2) The hill tribes should be encouraged to stop growing opium and find other sources of income sufficient to make their living which will

lead to self-sufficiency. Improvements to their farming techniques, farm products, marketing system and the promotion of other professions will help increase the income of the people. NGOs should be encouraged to take parts in the hill tribe development.

(3) Health-care service should be provided in as many communities as possible. Basic health care should be improved and treatment for drug addicts be promoted.

(4) Family planning must be adopted to control the highland population birth rate. This will keep the balance between population numbers and natural resource availability.

(5) Both formal and non-formal primary education should be provided so as to form the foundation for future communications, socio-economic development, political administration and natural resource conservation.

(6) Buddhism be promoted among the tribal societies so as to build up national unity. Missionaries of other religions be supervised to be sure that they do not create conflicts among the people which could affect national development.

2.2 Opium growing and use

(1) The people should be told of the danger of opium growing and smoking (through propaganda and other psychological approaches).

(2) Legal action be taken especially in the areas

which have been officially recognised and developed.

(3) Aid be sought from foreign organizations for the solution of drug problems in the highlands (and also to help Thai addicts)

3. Natural resource: usage, conservation and development

(1) Land use plans should be made in order to help conserve and develop natural resources in the highlands. The plan is to be strictly followed under close control.

(2). Legal restrictions and laws regarding natural resources are to be taken seriously.

The organizations resposible for hill tribe work are:

1. National level : the National Security Committee on the hill tribes and opium affairs.

2. Regional level: The Third Army (the committee of hill tribe affairs and the eradication of opium growing)

3. Provincial level : the provincial committee of hill tribe affairs.

4. District level : the district committee of hill tribe affairs.

Thailand, unlike other countries with minorities, does not have a specific Ministry or department which works directly with the minorities.

However, the government is considering establishing one department to work specifically on hill tribe affairs.

Department of Public Welfare's work

Since 1959,the DPW has been working in accordance with the National Policy on Hill Tribe as follows :

1) Acting as a committee member and secretary to the Central Hill Tribe Committee 1959-1982.

2) Making plans and conducting welfare work for the hill tribe, namely:

- Setting up 4 self-help settlement projects (Nikhoms), starting in 1960.

- Setting up mobile units for hill tribe welfare work in the key and satellite villages, working under the Provincial Hill Tribe Welfare Centre. There are at the moment 13 centres.

- Proposal of "Integratiom Policy" in 1976 so as to make the hill tribes become good and self-sufficient Thai citizens through the zonal integrated development.

3) Setting up the Hill Tribe Welfare Division in 1963.

4) Research and survey work.

4.1 First survey on socio-economic in 1961-1962.

4.2 Founding of the Tribal Research Centre in1965 in cooperation with Chiang Mai University.

The centre became the **Tribal Research Institute** acting as advisory division with useful information and findings of different researchers being used to help with the hill tribe work.

4.3 Cooperation with Australian experts and the Faculty of Agriculture of Chiang Mai University, in order to study old farm land which has been deserted by the hill tribes due to low soil fertility and weed problems in an attempt to find a way to refertilize the land for future use (either for cultivation, for cattle or for forestry).

5) Building up relationships with the hill tribes.

5.1 Promotion of Dhammajarik Project in 1965 (Buddhism promotion).

5.2 Cooperation with volunteer groups from different universities and NGOs.

6) Providing aid to other projects such as the Royal Project, the Substitute Crops (UN), the Non-formal Education Project, the Addiction Healing Project and other training projects. The Tribal Research Institute once has been approved to do a cartographic and socio-economic survey through a request from other organizations which made use of such information.

7) Acting as a base organization for foreign organizations which work in the highlands in cooperation with the Thai government, such as the Thai-Australian Project, the Thai-Norway Highland Development Project (which is supported by

Norwegian Church Aid) and Thai-German Highland Development Project.

8) Working on the eradication of opium growing, on addiction healing of various forms and on reafforestation in hill tribe villages.

9) Working on hill tribe censuses for future consideration of Thai nationality for the hill tribes.

(Source : Wanat Bhruksasri "Hill Tribes : Information and Figures" in *Hill Tribes : Ways of Life & Development*. Chiang Mai, Tribal Research Institute, 1991. p. 26-33)

FURTHER READINGS

Burling, R. (1965)   *Hill Farms and Paddy-Fields.*
Englewood Cliffs, New jersey, Prentice Hall.

Chindasri, Nusit (1976) *The Religion of the Hmong Njua.* Bangkok, Siam Society.

Cultural Survival, Inc. (1987) *Southeast Asian Tribal Groups and Ethnic Minorities.* Cambridge, Cultural Survival, Inc.

Department of the Army. (1970) *Minority Groups in Thailand : Ethnographic Study Series.* Department of the Army Pamphlet No. 550-770 Washington D.C. : U.S. Government Printing office.

Embree, J.F. (1950) *Ethnic Groups of Northern Souteast Asia.* Yale University Press.

Geddes W.R. (1976) *Migrants of the Mountains.* Clarendon Press, Oxford.

Grunfeld, Frederic V. (1982) *Wayfarers of the Thai Forest : The Akha.* Amsterdam, Time-Life Books.

Hamilton, J.W. (1976) *Pwo Karen at the Edge of Mountain and plain.* West Publishing.

Illustralted Encyclopedia of Mankind. (1978) V.1-20. London, Marshall Cavendish.

Kang, Tai S. editor. (1979) *Nationalism and The Crises of Ethnic Minorities in Asia.*London, Greenwood Press.

Keyes, Charles F. (1977) *The Golden Peninsula : Culture and Adaptation in Mainland . Southeast Asia.* New York, Macmillan; London, Collier Macmillan.

Keyes, Charles F. editor. (1979) *Ethnic Adaptation and Identity : the Karen on the Thai Frontier with Burma.* Philadelphia, Institute for the Study of Human Issues.

Kunstadter, P. editor. *SoutheastAsian Tribes, Minorities and Nations.* (2 Volumes) Princeton, Princeton University Press.

Kunstdter, P. Chapman, E.C. and Sanga Sabhasri,editors. (1978) *Farmers in the Forest,* Honolulu, University Press of Hawii.

Lemoine, Jecques. (1982) *Yao Ceremonial Paintings.* Bangkok : White Lotus. Co., Ltd.

Lebar, Frank M. Gerald C. Hickey and John K. Musgrave. (1964) *Ethnic Groups of Mainland Southeast Asia.* New Haven, Human Relations Area Files, Inc.,

Lewis, Paul W. (1969) *Ethnographic Notes on the Akha of Burma* (3 Volumes) New Haven,

Lewis, Paul W. and Paul Elaine. (1983) *People of the Golden Triangle.* Thames, Thames and Hudson.

Mckinnon, John and Wanat Brukasri, editors. (1983)
The Highlanders of Thailand. Kuala Lampur;
Oxford Univer sity press.

Mckinnon, John and Vienne, Bernard. (1987) *Hill Tribes
Today : problems in development.* Bangkok,
ORSTOM; White Lotus.

Mottin,Jean. (1980) *The History of the Hmong (Meo).*
Bangkok, Odean Store Ltd.

Saihoo, Patya. (1962) *The Hill Tribes of Northern
Thailand.* Bangkok, SEATO.

Srisavasdi, Boonchuey. (1963) *The Hill Tribes of Siam.*
Bangkok, Khun Aroon.

Tribal Research Centre. *Tribesmen and Peasants in
North Thailand.* Bangkok, Sompong Press Ltd.

Walker, Anthony R. Editor. (1975) *Farmers in the
Hills : Upland People of North Thailand.*
Penang University of Malaysia.

Walker, Anthony R. Editor. (1992) *The Highland Heritage* : Collected Essays on Upland North Thailand. Singapore, Suvarnabhumi Books.

Yong, Gordon. (1962) *The Hill Tribes of Northern Thailand* 2nd edition; Bangkok, The Siam Society.

- People and places in the hills.
- Over 5,000 copies sold in the past year....
- In its fourth Revised & Enlarged printed edition......
- Based on over 20 years of research........
- Value for money......

"An excellent summary of the current Thai sociology of hnowledge concerning the highlanders"

John McKinnon
Department of Geography
Victoria University of Wellington
New Zealand